BRITISH POLITICS!

What about the tax payer?

Scott MacKenzie

authorHOUSE®

AuthorHouse™ UK Ltd.
500 Avebury Boulevard
Central Milton Keynes, MK9 2BE
www.authorhouse.co.uk
Phone: 08001974150

First published by AuthorHouse 6/19/2009

ISBN: 978-1-4389-8176-5 (sc)

This book is printed on acid-free paper.

CONTENTS

Introduction

IT ONLY TAKES SO MUCH for a normal person to get to the end of his tether. The problem is that you have reached this point so many times, but you say to yourself, what can I do? So you piss and moan, but nothing ever changes. I have been there more times than I can remember, and I'm only twenty-nine.

I have no chance of making the changes I want to make, because let's be fair, I never went to Oxford or Cambridge. However, here is the thing.

Every person who is head of a family runs a budget. Although far more simple than the government's budget, it's not much different. The government has a total revenue and must make everything work using that amount of money.

What happens is this: from the past, the government thinks certain issues bother people like you and me (and maybe because of how we are conditioned, we think they do), but in reality, if you thought about it, the real thing that matters is how well your family lives.

Charity starts at home, they say, so why is it okay for you to struggle on through life barely making ends meet? You pay your tax money, and let's think about this: every time you buy something, those thieves get something from you so you can't ever afford any luxuries. You are all but managing to survive, yet the family down the road has realised they are all better off if they never lift a finger. They are better off on benefits; they sit on their asses laughing at you because you go out at seven o'clock in the morning and don't come back till seven o'clock at night. All they think about is what film to watch on television and who is walking down the shop with *your money* to buy them fags or booze.

I am going out on a limb here and saying that surely you are as annoyed as I am. It's time to get real! It is my hope and belief that all people who work and support this country feel cheated and helpless to change things. Maybe we are, but by writing this book, I hope that millions of you will see the light and we all will stand united and take back the right our ancestors fought for, to have our say and get the standard of living we deserve.

(I) Who Funds This Country?

The answer to this question is very simple: the working person!

There are three political parties. the Conservative Party represents the middle class and the rich, the Labour Party represents the working class, and the Liberal Party represents the people who hate the conservatives and the labour. Let's be fair. Why do the Liberal Democrats even bother? They will never get in, not in a million years. Your choice is between two, and no matter whom you vote for and what they say, nothing is ever going to get better. Why, you ask? I will tell you: because they fight about rubbish! Do you watch the news, see the politicians in the House of Commons, and think that it's anything but great entertainment? It's funny, but does any of that give me a better standard of living? No, of course it doesn't. But the parties are programmed to fight about these policies because society dictates that that is what they do. Or does it?

I say, why doesn't the government or shadow government ask the people what they want, what issues really affect their lives, and what would make a difference to the taxpayer?

They never will, and you know why. The reason is that they will never be challenged. This country has become so consumed with what is expected to matter that the people we rely on to run it are too blinkered to even take stock of how our lives are or how hard things are out here. We are in a recession. Oh no! Do you know what this means? My interpretation is this: those competent people running our country have spent too much money ignoring the backbone of people, so that now you and I will have to become even poorer to get things back on track by putting up tax, etc., to recoup vital funds.

(II) Legalised Theft

What an interpretation! I call it this for very certain reasons.

Everyone reading this book has seen one version of Robin Hood.

Politicians make it legal to take our money, money that we work our asses off to earn, and run the country with it. But here is the thing, what do they spend this money on and what do we get from it? The answer is simple. *We get nothing!*

The richer you are, the harder you work, and the more that is stolen from you.

How much you earn is insignificant because every person is in the same boat. Everyone in this country that works knows that at the end of the month when they get their wages, a large portion will be legally stolen from them. Now, who would mind if you got something back? But, in reality, you get poorer so the dregs of society can exist among us. Let's be honest, because the poor drain us as they do, there is more crime, more teenage pregnancy, more kids causing problems hanging around where we live, and more drains on the resources of this country. I for one have had enough. What will it take for something to change?

I know what some say. Let's open up more youth centres so they have somewhere to go and plan crime. Let's make it known that if you get pregnant, we will support you. When you break the law, don't worry; the prisons are so full that we will waste money rehabilitating you when, in reality, you are always going to be a loser, a pest and problem of society, and a thorn in the good person's side.

I say we need to bring back classes. If you are poor, tough; be poor. Everyone has a shot at an education in this country. If you don't want one, who cares? Try a life of crime; you will go to jail and rot there.

I don't care about you, and if I were prime minister, I would tell you as much. The taxpayer in this country is no longer funding you; for all I care, you can starve. Harsh, but without motivation, when will these people get any better? Don't pat them on the back and feel sorry for them; kick them up the ass and make them some use! Better still: stop these scumbags having kids they can't afford!

Why do the people that work hard get no rewards?

Another simple answer! Because the people I have just been slagging off get all our tax money, about £60 billion to be precise. This figure sounds like a lot, but to put it in context, the waste of time NHS costs us the same.

Let me tell you something.

In America, there is no National Health. But, what happens to the people who can't afford private medical insurance?

I'll tell you, they go to clinics, which give them the minimum treatment required for their injury. They are fools for it, because it costs for a family of four a mere $150, that's £75 a month. Do you know how much your PAYE is? Shocking, isn't it? This is the main reason why our standard of living is so poor. Believe me, if we got rid of the NHS and paid private health insurance, each person in this country would be four grand a year better off on average.

Let's let the lazy gits suffer!

Chapter 1
Why I Am Writing This Book

HERE IS THE THING. I am now a successful twenty-nine-year-old man. I have achieved more than my life's ambitions, and because I am a real guy, I realise this fact. (Here today, gone tomorrow.) This is why I am voicing my opinion in this capacity. While I write this book, I wonder if it will ever be published. As I'm typing, I know how it will go, and I know I will annoy a lot of people. But this thought is making me chuckle while it's in my head, as I consider all the people that this book will piss off. Apart from the politicians who won't buy it because of the title, why would scroungers who do not care about anything but a free ride even consider buying this book? They will just glance at the title and think nothing of it; that's assuming they can even read! I know I sound bitter, and I am. I'm now thinking that if I wasn't writing and venting my views, I wouldn't be as relaxed as I feel right now, as relaxed as I feel every time I get my little fingers on this laptop.

Now I am going to move on to my extreme, but I hope widespread, opinions on this country.

Chapter 2
What Is Democracy?

DEMOCRACY IS THE POLITICAL ORIENTATION of those who favour government by the people or by their elected representatives.

It is a political system in which the supreme power lies in a body of citizens who can elect people to represent them through majority rule.

It is the doctrine that the numerical majority of an organized group can make decisions binding on the whole group.

What does it mean to you and me? Well, I would like to think that as taxpayers, our views would be cared about because, after all, we are the people who vote in these political representatives.

The reality is this: we never get to change anything. We have local MPs we can talk to about little issues we need help with, but what about the real issues that are argued about in the House of Commons? How do we voice our opinions about those issues?

I have written to the PM three times and never once have he or his delegates had the common courtesy to even acknowledge my letters. I ask myself why. Very simple. No one who runs this country can possibly do anything outside the box just in case he doesn't appeal to the so-called majority. Think about that; the only reason people vote is because they are told lies around election time. When nothing they are promised happens, what can they do? They're stuck with these politicians for four more years.

But then, four years later, who do they vote for? Politicians are all the same. You really don't have a choice, do you? So you just go with the party you have always gone with, and I bet that's the party your family has always supported. What a vicious circle politics has become. Now, tell me how this country is a democracy.

Chapter 3
Lies

I TOUCHED ON THIS WORD in the previous chapter, but because of the very word I'm talking about and how it affects all our lives in so many ways, not just in politics, I thought it deserved its own chapter.

I'm sure everyone reading this book has been lied to at some point in their lives, whether it be by friends, partners, or kids.

How do you react? Is it okay, or do you get upset by it? Sometimes, it can ruin your life for a period, but like all things, you get over it and move on. Things get better because that person who lied to you makes it up to you and that in turn earns forgiveness.

Politicians, on the other hand, have been lying to us and cheating us out of a good lifestyle for far too long. Not only that, but they don't even make it up to us. I never remember getting anything from them but more tax and less money in my pocket.

So this begs the question, why do we put up with it?

The answer is because we have no choice. How does the average man in the street say enough is enough and be heard by anyone who has the position or power to make the changes needed to help him get the life he deserves?

He can't. No one cares that he works his ass off to make ends meet and, God forbid, have a few luxuries, which are all taxed to the hilt.

Chapter 4

Has Any Politician Got Balls?

WHAT DO I MEAN BY this question? I'll tell you. When you choose the path of politics, to my mind, you have to be intelligent for starters or you wouldn't get the necessary qualifications for the main panel of politicians to listen to you and allow you into their party. Let's be fair; if you want a career in this industry, you have to join Tories or Labour.

In reality, why do you bother? To me, politics would be for a person who wanted to make a difference. Let's take a charity worker, for example. Look at the way that person puts himself out for what he believes in and then look at a politician. All politicians do is cleverly skate around issues and leave more answers to questions asked of them; they know that if they tell an intelligent interviewer what the real story is, they will be made out to be, and proved to be, the very waste of space they really are. I say we change the way people who represent us are given opportunity. Who better to run this country, or any country, than retired business people who have worked their asses off to support our economy all their lives?

Tell me how someone born with a silver spoon in his mouth, who enjoyed the privilege of the best education available, who has never really worked to achieve anything or struggled to survive in real life, or who has never been around people who can give him a slight insight into the things that really matter to the working people of this great country possibly qualify to be in a position of power in politics.

Balls are the real thing that matters in life and especially in a democracy like ours. Here's the thing; if you had as many great ideas as I do, ideas that would really make the lives of the people that matter better, how and when would you take these ideas forward? Easy, you'd go to the House of Commons. Trouble is, if you did, your clique might not like you anymore. So, I know, let's just be sheep and keep in with the out-of-touch idiots that can further our careers, because after all, we only care about ourselves and our own lifestyles, not the taxpayer or his lifestyle. My job is not to fight for what is right; it is to speak up when I feel I'm agreeing with the majority so I won't be an outcast. Well, if that's the case, I say anybody can be a politician.

When was the last time one of those MPs was on the news and actually made any sense or actually explained something so you could understand? They are taught to talk rubbish and to use words most of us don't understand. Why? So we think that we could never do their job because they are so much more intelligent than we are. Here is the thing. I am twenty-nine years old and considerably richer than that 'one-eyed Scottish idiot' who runs our country, as Jeremy Clarkson put it. By the way, what a legend Jeremy Clarkson is, what a very apt description that is, and if only he'd said more. Thank you, Jeremy. You are the main reason I am writing this book, as your whole personality is so motivational. Trust me; you are a prime candidate to run this country, and if I had your money, I would make it happen.

So the guy who runs this country makes £100,000, say. I personally know ten uneducated people that make more than that amount and, in fact, probably get robbed of more than his salary in tax. But does he know more than they do? Not a chance. Running this country is no different from running a business, so why don't we get a businessman to do it? The time is now to get rid of the do-gooders. If you want to help the lazy, do it with your own money and stop spending ours. With your pathetic ideas and lies, you have been exposed; get real. The new faction will have balls, and once this book comes out, you will all be in the dole queue. And guess what? No one will ever employ you because you are a waste of our polluted air. *Oh no!* It's 2009, and we have snow; the planet is finished. Have you forgotten 1976? Shut up, you fools. I see you for what you are. Let's save the planet, and I'll tell you how. Let's make gas and electric so expensive that people can't afford it, and petrol, too, to mention a few. How the hell do you thieves get away with it? It's time to stop you and, may God be my witness, I am annoyed and I will change things for the better. Although the weather is bad, I love this country. If you people that have the power won't fight for us, I sure as hell will. None of you have any of the qualifications I think are relevant for the job you have, and it's time you were shown up for what you really are. Your days are numbered. You forgot about your taxpayers, and they should be the first thing you care about and fight to defend. You are a joke!

Chapter 5

Why Do We Put Up with It?

I REALLY DON'T KNOW. IT'S taken me this long to get so pissed off. I have taken the only action as an uneducated businessman in this country I believe I can take to start a little revolution against these people.

I got a letter the other day from a company called Who's Who. The reason behind this letter was that of things like Dragons Den. I was being recognized as one of Britain's youngest directors with a net worth of over £5,000, a very small amount of money; but what a lovely piece of mail.

I felt good, but it just reminded me of how much money I put into this country and how little I get back. If I was Richard Branson, I am sure I would have done something so extreme by now because I have had enough. Only God can imagine how someone that rich and successful must feel, yet he takes life in such a calm fashion. How is that man so chilled and so optimistic? Maybe he knows something we don't know.

I am straight down the line; however, I am fast approaching dodgy, and wish I knew how to get a bit back without breaking the law.

Yes, we as the British public have put up with more than I care to explain compared to other countries. I really feel that is so because, although we are skeptical, we have faith in people and most of us see the best in people no matter how many times we get screwed over. When will we take heed from other races and stick up for ourselves? Why do the British not stick together? We are too consumed with keeping up with the Joneses and so competitive that we want to see each other fail. We are all suffering because of it.

I moved abroad three years ago to complete a business project I was very excited about and an example of what I just said follows.

I was on a certain high street trying to speak to a woman with no translator and, in fairness, she spoke three languages that I knew very little of. I saw a lady who spoke my language and the woman's, and asked her to help me very briefly, only to get some fat, selfish English woman about sixty go mad at this girl and say, 'You work for me. Don't ever translate for anybody else.' I found this quite shocking. I, therefore, went crazy at this silly cow and with that, she got quite offended and threatened me with her husband. I, being a young fit guy with lots of confidence, said, 'Bring it on, you stupid woman.' With that, her rather fat husband came around the corner rather apologetic, realising that should he start on me, I would destroy him. He said very little. I then pointed out that should we as a nation in a strange country not try to screw each other and stick together, we could all do well just like, for instance, the people from Pakistan do because they stick together and help each other.

I think that our wonderful leaders use this behaviour against us and try to instill into us that this is the appropriate behaviour, because they want the country split. So when election time comes, it is a very close contest and a very competitive affair, when in reality, no one is offering anything that will help us. They are just trying to secure their chance to be the forefront of the country. I mean, what a buzz being number one. Becoming the prime minister; what an achievement.

How can we let these people think this? This job comes with so much responsibility and its time they realised this. We vote and in reality, we have no choice, whichever way this goes nothing will ever change because no matter what we think they will do what they were taught at University and completely ignore their responsibility as a leader of our great country.

So once again, I ask, why do we put up with this? Please get mad and stop giving these people your support. I have a very good feeling that this book will change things and believe me if it doesn't I give up cause what else can a guy like me do!

Chapter 6
This Is a Dictatorship; We Just Vote for the Dictator

WHAT A STATEMENT, WHEN YOU consider what a dictatorship is like. Look at the recent wars in which we have participated.

Iraq was being run by Saddam, and he was a total mental case. However, what was the real motive behind that involvement from the Western world? I'll tell you: *oil*. I am proud of Britain, and God, I love the American people, but their government only got involved because they knew that, as a united force, the opposition would be very easily defeated. Obviously, the Americans and we would suffer casualties, but all in all, those people that laid down their very valuable lives for the people in power were worth losing because we could get control of the oil fields in the Far East. We would do so by placing a democracy in the country that would sell oil to us cheap; therefore, we'd have a plentiful oil supply and screw over the British by taking the piss on tax. At least Americans only wanted it to protect their amazingly cheap prices. Good for you, America. You look after your taxpayers, even if your motives are a little extreme.

What about Africa then? This is 2009, and the Western world has stolen all the precious things this now very poor continent once had, yet we haven't declared war on President Mugabe who is stealing all the basic rights from his people. I might add that the majority of this money is from the Western world. Are these tortured people not worth our help? All I hear is a lot of threats, and I see no action. It's one man for God's sake, and let's not forget: he lost the election but is still in power. The reason we have not interfered is because this war would actually be for a good purpose, for the sake of basic human rights. But what profit does that have for the superpowers of this world? As I just said, this is 2009, and people in this world have no water and no food! Millions die every day, and this tragedy has been going on for years. How do the world leaders let this happen? It's shocking. Remember when the tsunami happened? That huge tragedy was no worse than the plight of daily life in North Africa, yet because it happened in a tourist zone, the funds earmarked were colossal. Am I the only one who can see these points and the only one who cares? Of course not, but the people who can change things do nothing, or if they do something, they do the bare minimum.

Are we so different in leadership from the Middle East, where the dictatorship is in force? We're different because we are not so thick as to believe that we will go to a better place by walking into a packed place with a bomb strapped to our backs and kill one hundred Western people. But let's not forget that these countries do not have a superior air force to drop bombs, etc., to kill one hundred of their people. Never mind what our morals say. I believe that we only attack things we have to, to tactically remove impending threats.

But, and what a big but this is, if the Quran tells these people that it is okay to do this type of thing, then why the hell are we letting them build their mosques in our country? I have no problem with anyone's beliefs, but ask yourself this. Are we allowed to build a church in Iraq or wear the clothes we choose without getting mobbed? No, and yet people can live in our backyard and wear a headscarf that totally covers their identity. How would you feel if everyone started wearing balaclavas? How intimidated would you feel? So why do we allow things that make us uncomfortable here at home, when if we went to the Far East, we would be told how to dress? Something ain't right here. My philosophy is, each to his own, but when it's one rule for one and the goalposts change in their country, I'm not down with that.

So what I'm saying to this politically correct government is be there for us, stop giving these people a break until they return the favour, and live and let live. They must exist by our beliefs; if not, they must go home. We don't want extremists here; we are peaceful people. If your religion dictates terrorism, stay where you are. But, do the world a favour and stop picking on your own people. It's a crime, you sadistic bastards! Human life is very valuable. It's time the world's people stopped killing each other. Racism is a very serious problem in the world, but religion in general does itself no favours. When is the last time you heard about an atheist killing anybody? In my opinion, which is very personal and humble, I don't knock what anybody clings onto to make this sick world a better place, but keep those beliefs to yourself. If all you want is to cause pain and suffering to innocent people, surely you have to question what you are really doing. Do these people that get hurt really deserve it? *No! Think* who is getting something out of this, and I am talking to all sides. I have friends from every walk of life. Do I want to hurt them? No, because I love them for who they are, not for what they were brought up to believe; that is their personal business. Take heed, world; I am making sense. There are no enemies, just different beliefs. Stop fighting each other off. Let's expel the evil in this world and live together in harmony.

Chapter 7

The Budget: *Think!*, When Is the Last Time Something Was Good for You?

THE BUDGET! **WHAT IS THIS** complete load of flannel? You can be sure every year things go up. No matter what is televised and how miniscule some savings are, the reality is that that the average man will fail to notice how many things are made more expensive. Fair play when the chancellor finally reveals his master plan, and God, he puts some effort into making you think you're better off. We will more than likely moan, and in the majority, the cost of fags, petrol, and booze will go up.

Are we that narrow minded? Yes, because it's so boring that that is the only thing we really hear. Do you think for one minute the government will even remotely stick to the budget? Of course not! Why would the budget be honored? You don't take notes, and you only watch the summary on the news, so you really have no idea if it's good or bad anyway. The budget is a bit like a business plan that you take to the bank to borrow money so you can fund a new venture; but there's one major difference. We have no choice on whether we give the money or not; it's the law to pay our taxes. This means that the chancellor works out roughly how much he will steal from his taxpayers, how much he will pay out to run the country, and how much he will spend on the things that we don't want him to spend the money on. Hopefully, he will have some money left to pay off some of the national debt. Ideally, of course, he will have funds left for emergencies and things that tend to crop up a bit; just as when our car breaks down. What a nightmare that is!

So, going back to the title of this chapter, why every year do we have less and less money in our pocket and are worse off, yet nothing in this country gets any better? I'm confused. Surely if there is more money in the pot, things improve. This never being the case just begs the question, where does the money go? Ten years ago, fags were £1.50 and the average wage was £10,000. Now fags are £5.00 and the average wage is the same. That's just one perfect example of the sheer mismanagement of our money. How, I ask you then, when we are all so skint and the government has so much more of our money, have we gone into recession?

This means that we will need to find more public money to get the government out of the shit. Where will the money come from, I ask you? Our pockets, that's where! This is another reason that we need to try to change our mentality and protect our rights. Let's stop the constant lies and help ourselves. If we don't, and those selfish, deceitful MPs sure won't, then who will?

Chapter 8
Cost of Living

THIS IS A LOVELY FOLLOW-ON chapter from the one you just read, as it gives me the chance to put to you the very thing that annoys me the most. I would like to look at the history of how the cost of living has changed over the last twenty years, 1989 to 2009. Let's split this chapter in two sections, one for each year. We will take the average person and his situation to make our comparison.

I—1989

Prime Minister: Margaret Thatcher
Party: Conservative
Unemployment rate: 7.2 percent
Inflation rate: 7.8 percent
Interest rates: 15 percent
Average wage: £7,975
Average property price across UK: £36,284
Average price for a loaf of bread: 48p
Average price for a pint of beer: 87p

Average price for a litre of petrol: 41p
Average price for a pack of cigarettes: £1.50
Most popular car: Ford Escort
(sourced from uk.answers.yahoo.com)

II—2009

I would just like to say here I have been searching 2009 data for two hours with no results to show you. What a surprise. I think if anyone published anything on this subject, they would lose the will to live. Perhaps we don't want to know, but I do, and I will bring you some information, because it is very important for this book.

Prime Minister: Gordon Brown
Party: Labour
Unemployment rate: 7.2 percent
Inflation rate: 3 percent
Interest rates: 1.5 percent
Average wage: £22'000; but, in reality, most people earn between £11,000 and £16,000
Average property price across UK: £190,000
Average price for a loaf of bread: £1.12
Average price for a pint of beer: £2.75
Average price for a litre of petrol: £1.00
Average price for a pack of cigarettes: £6.00
Most popular car: Who Cares?
(sourced from uk.answers.yahoo.com)

So to compare each of these things goes like this

1. Unemployment remains the same.
2. Inflation is down 65 per cent
3. Interest rates are supposedly 1 per cent or thereabout, but who can borrow money at this rate? I'm paying 6.7 per cent, so does that mean this rate is a just a make-believe figure, so no one in this country can actually afford to borrow? Of course it is! Let's not forget this is now a credit crunch, and no one is lending any money. It's a bit like showing a man dying of thirst in the desert an ice cold glass of water, then pouring it in the sand, jumping on your camel, and speeding off leaving him to suck wet sand and die while laughing as you drink some lovely water yourself.
4. Wages are up 275 per cent, if the average wage really is 22,000; but I don't believe this figure, do you?
5. Property is up over 500 per cent, so even if wages *were* up 275 per cent, house prices are up double on wages. How is that right? No wonder no one can get on the housing ladder. Before people think, 'yes, but now our house is worth more than it ever was.' they should remember it's all relative unless you sell, go into rented, or move abroad. It's no benefit to you because if you sell your house and move next door, it will be the same price, so you will have gained nothing by your house going up anyway. I think it's just a way of the government getting more stamp duty when you do move.
6. The good old loaf of bread that people used to steal to feed their family, I would have stole a juicy steak for the punishment doled out in the olden days for such

a petty crime. Well, that basic cheap and staple food has risen 250 per cent, just in line with your wages, so not that bad, eh?

7. Beer, one of the old favourites to moan about in the budget, is up a whopping 315 per cent. Well, why not, after all? Why should the good old working man have a nice cold pint after work or on the weekends after a hard week? I mean, anything in life enjoyable surely should be taxed to the hilt so we can't have a bit of fun to break our mundane existence, not at the mercy of the chancellor and his one-eyed pal that used to do his job. Assholes!

8. Petrol is up 250 per cent. This is my favourite, as it is not a pleasure but a necessity. We all need it to get to work so we can pay our taxes to the thieves. We all need it to get our children to school or to the hospital or the doctors. We need it to do the shopping. We need it for just about everything we do.

    We use petrol even to mow our tiny little gardens. Here is the thing, though; what about the haulage industry, one of the backbones of British industry? How many more businesses will have to go bust because they can't afford the tax on fuel? Do you remember a few years ago when the fuel strikes were on? Our farmers and truckers put their hearts and spirits on the line to stand up and say, 'We cannot afford this anymore. You are taking the food from our families' mouths.' So we all went without fuel until the government said, 'Right! Let's send out our private little army, the police, to arrest these hardworking people.' Of course, these were just the very people standing up for us that were moaning about the prices in the first place.

The government could have put prices down. Politicians knew they were crippling people, but they didn't give a toss. Well, there is another example for you. Just well I remember a head of a bank bailed out by taxpayers' money; he retired yesterday, and his annual pension is... wait for it... 600,000 per year! *What?* That guy has done nothing but fleece us his whole career and we are paying him that wage? Well, I'll tell you this, big boy. When I get in, that wage will be reduced to the state pension. Unless you have private pensions, you had better come out of retirement and get a job in ASDA. That is taking the piss, and I think you know it; you failed, and if it weren't for the government bailing you out with *our* money, you would have nothing because your bank would be bust. That goes for the rest of you, too, and extends to any politician. You are messing up our economy, so forget your pensions. You ain't getting them! Look out!

9. Cigarettes are up 400 per cent. Well, I have already said a few things on this topic, so I don't want to go on too much. Plus, I am saving a bit back for my chapter on the NHS, so let's just agree that this increase is awful big and needs to be reduced.

Chapter 9
The Leeches of Society

WHILE RESEARCHING THE ABOVE CHAPTER on the internet, I just so happened to stumble across this little article I thought I had to copy and paste for you all to see. It's just another example of this stupid government, refusing to admit how it is encouraging people to claim benefits because it's so god dam easy.

Benefits more lucrative than average wage
Monday, December 29, 2008

Tory Chris Grayling has criticised the number of families receiving more in state benefits than the average take-home wage

Some 140,000 families are raking in more in benefits than the average take-home salary, it

has been revealed.

The households are pocketing more than £20,000 in handouts every year, according to official estimates.

The scale of the payments is likely to anger millions of families struggling to cope with the fallout from the economic downturn.

The average salary before tax is just over £25,000, but after deductions that sum shrinks to just over £19,000. In contrast, benefits are tax-free.

Employment minister Tony McNulty insisted the 140,000 represented just 1% of households with at least one person of working age. He said: 'The benefits being received by these households will, in the majority of cases, include disability-related benefits and premiums.'

But shadow work and pensions Secretary Chris Grayling, who obtained the information using parliamentary questions, said the number was still 'an awful lot.' Many families would be receiving tens of thousands of pounds in housing benefit alone, he added.

Work and Pensions Secretary James Purnell announced radical plans this month to get millions off benefits and into work, including reforming incapacity benefit and forcing lone parents to seek employment.

A Department for Work and Pensions spokesman said: 'These families are a tiny minority and in almost all cases the money includes extra support for the most severely disabled. Our welfare reforms are about ensuring almost everyone will have to do something for their benefits, but we are not going to apologise for supporting those disabled people who need help most.'

A spokesman for Mr Purnell accused Mr Grayling of 'posturing' over welfare.

"The Tories are happy for drug addicts to get benefits with no questions asked and have opposed our plans to ask workless parents to take active steps to prepare for work in return for financial support, but now seem to be saying they don't think families struggling to cope with a disability should get real help," he said. 'It's time Chris Grayling got serious on welfare reform and, instead of posturing, backed our proposals to ask more from those who receive benefits.

(sourced from metro.co.uk)

Well, there is a prime example of politicians arguing with each other about things that really matter, but nothing ever changes. They are more interested in scoring points off each other than listening to one another and working out something that will help the taxpayer.

Let's take this argument and strip it down. Each and every taxpayer will have sympathy for the less fortunate that have real disabilities and do need the support of others to get by. But so many fake these ailments, claim benefits, and get away with it. I won't go on, but one example is depression. Are you serious? I should give over my stressfully earned money to some depressed scab? I'll tell you what, go kill yourself; it will be less of a strain on the taxpayer; or, better still, pull yourself together and get on with life. My cousin has lost two children, and he still goes out to work and supports his family. Hard as it may be, he claims nothing! Get a grip; we are not paying for you anymore.

So in conclusion of this point, there are genuine cases and fraudulent cases; let's just agree to wheedle them out.

The £20,000 per year may include the disabled, so let's half it so we can take the normal scroungers into account. You know who they are, the lazy ones from the council estates that sit on their arses all day because they can, the ones who never bothered at school because they didn't give a shit about a future for themselves or their family, the ones who have babies constantly because then they never have to dig into their pockets to support them. Those people, and yes, they can be male or female. They get £10,000per year from us and put back nothing into this country.

The article above says that the average wage is £25,000with a take-home wage of £19,000after income tax, not forgetting the tax or VAT on absolutely everything we buy. I wonder how much the government steals from every pound in the UK that goes through our hands. I'll hazard a guess of 65 per cent. No way, you say! I bet research somewhere states I'm not far off. I employ six people, and by the way, as an employer, I have to pay the government tax just to employ them. Yet another piss take!

The average wage at my company is £15,000, a far cry from the £25,000the national average is stating. So by working for me, and this is in the financial services industry for forty hours a week, employees only earn the same as the scroungers on benefits, after income tax and National Insurance (NI).

No wonder people are claiming benefits! To top their benefits, they might do a bit of crime, maybe some cash-in-hand work, more than likely. They are better off than my staff, who are honest, hardworking people. I'm sorry, but calling all those on benefits: when I get things right, you will still get your benefits, thank God, you say, but you will be working forty hours a week for the government. You will be cleaning the streets, cleaning the graphite off the walls that your kids have just put there, and doing any other jobs we will line up for you. You will work to save the government money, to justify your meaningless existence, and to avoid our country's money being wasted. Here's the thing. I give you a month, and you will be signed off the dole and working for a living, aspiring to this average wage of £25,000.

As for the Tories being happy to fund drug addicts, you silly Labour politician man, is that the best comeback you could manage? The Tories, in case you forgot, are for the middle class to upper class. I'm sure they don't want to fund any of the scum of society the Labour government has been funding for the last ten years. The drug addicts are obviously a major problem, so lock them up. Then they can't commit crime or take drugs. It's not rocket science. It will save us a fortune on policing them and spending money on rehab. In fact, I bet if you put them in jail, it would be a damn site cheaper than a rehab clinic. I'm not talking about these prisons that are really country clubs with TV, etc. I'm talking the Midnight Express prison: overpopulated and filthy, where criminals can reflect on what they have done and hope to God they will never go back to the shit hole where they have found themselves. You never know. If prison was a tough as it should be, we might get a few suicides, and that would keep the cost right down and the scum off the streets.

I just wanted to give you one final thought on this subject. A girl I know who is on benefits told me this the other day, and I bet it will annoy you just as much as it did me.

If you're over your overdraft and you're employed, your wages go in to your account and, quite rightly, the bank takes back what you owe and takes a charge. But, if you're on benefits and you go over your overdraft, when *our* money goes into that lazy shit's account, you can still draw the whole lot! What a surprise! The working man gets done again.

Chapter 10

A New Start, New Ideas, and New Solutions to the Problems

SO FAR, I HAVE HAD plenty of things bad to say about society and the way the country is run, but I say there are never problems, only solutions.

What the hell do we do then? Let's start again. How about we start our own political party? Oh my God, what does this involve? I'll be honest; I could research this for you, but what is the point? Until this book has been published and enough of us taxpayers choose this course of action, I'm wasting my time. If, as a united front of taxpayers, we could get an expert to research it free because he believes in making things better for all of us. We all have our talents, and research is not one of mine. I find it very boring and time-consuming. So let's get down to the nitty gritty.

In the following chapters, you will see most of the political issues that I believe are important to us, the average people in this country, or the issues in the forefront of political arguments.

Chapter 11
Schools

THERE ARE TWO TYPES OF schools, public and private. Many children who show a great talent, no matter their background often get a scholarship to a very good private school, but the rest of the places go to children whose parents can afford it or to other parents who are comfortable but struggle their asses off to give their child that great education public school just does not offer. So what is the difference between the two? Well, I had my oldest in private school, and although she is not amazingly academic, she excelled because of the work ethic instilled into these children and the fact that the class sizes are small. Also, all children in these schools, whether they like it or not, learn, because when you spend money on your child's education, you make sure you encourage them to do well.

So say you put your child in private school. To my mind, you are not using the public education system. The education you are paying for would be tax deductible then, wouldn't it? Wrong; no tax relief. What about, then, if I have three children in public school and my neighbor only has one; why should he not get a little bit of relief because his family is costing the government less? These are silly points, you say, and maybe you're right. Don't forget the fact that our public schools are not good enough, as proven because this is a major talking point in politics.

The reality of our education system is this: schools are not much different from the real world. Some kids want to learn, and some don't. The ones that don't are often badly behaved and disruptive; they bully other children who want to learn, and waste the teacher's time on keeping them in line when the teacher's time is far better spent teaching children that want to get the most from their time at school, as my view is. It's law that you have to go to school, so while you're there, you may as well learn.

How many of us look back, wish we had paid attention, and regret not getting the best from our school days? If you were honest with yourself, could you say you have the job you always wanted or are you happy every day you go to work? Probably not.

So what do we do about it then? Do we just throw more and more money at it and hope it gets better? Yes, the government says. It's not our money, so why should we care? Well, I say no! Let's change things back to how they used to be. I always say, if it's not broken, don't fix it. Bring back grammar schools and secondary modern. You might ask why, and the answer is simple. At eleven years old, when students take their eleven plus, we find out who is going be academic and who isn't. We, therefore, can direct the kids in the right way. The ones who pass get a standard education; they will be with other kids that want to learn and will more than likely go to college and then university. That will be a good use of public money. The children who don't pass will be the ones who can't cope with learning and, therefore, will hate school, disrupt everyone else, and just stroll through achieving nothing at the end.

I say these kids, when they start secondary modern, should learn basic life skills, and, of course, reading, writing, and basic education. But also, we can find out what their talent is and give them the skills they need to do well in life. Why make children go to school with kids that are doing well when they themselves feel useless? Teach them to build houses or fix cars; give them a future early, not when they are sixteen and have a choice on whether they go to college or not. Kids will be kids; they won't bother, and then we have more benefit claimers. Give all children confidence and an equal chance in life. Hope is a very powerful emotion. They all deserve a slice of it, wouldn't you agree?

Chapter 12
The NHS

MY FAVOURITE ISSUE IS THE NHS. No one has got the guts to say anything radical in politics. All anyone does is pick fault with certain issues and problems. It's the perfect thing for the two parties to row about in the House of Commons or on *This Week*.

Nearly everything in this country has been privatised, apart from that pathetic black hole of an NHS. Why did we sell off all the things that made money and hang on to something that is impossible to run? Let's look at the BUPA chain and why they make money when all their members only pay £50 a month. Private care is one hundred times better than the NHS. There are no waiting lists, and the hospitals are clean.

Oh, my God! I have found the answer; we sell off the hospitals to the private sector. But why would we do this, you ask? I'll tell you why. The NHS, as I said before, costs us £60 billion a year, and that is four grand per head. What a joke! If we all paid private health insurance of say

£50 a month or what I'm paying (£95 for my family of five), that would cost the average family £1140 per year, a far cry from four grand each year.

But, what about the people who don't work? What happens to them? I'll tell you, we don't treat them. Is that cruel? I don't think so, and here is the reason. I wrote a long chapter (Chapter 9) called 'The Leeches of Society,' saying that all those on benefits would still get benefits but would work for the government. So if they work for the country, we will pay for their medical insurance. Once they get a job, as I said, they would pay it, as they would not work forty hours a week for dole money; their employer would pay for their medical insurance.

So the only people we have to worry about are the pensioners. Okay then, let's start from today. Anyone who reaches retirement and is on state pension for the next ten years gets free medical treatment subsidised by the government. We all know it's coming, so let's put things in place to cover your insurance for your old age. All working people pay something called NI (National Insurance). This will be the county hospital fund that I will use for the people that have no insurance and for the retired people. If you don't work and you are injured, we will save your life, and then you're on your own. This means you will get the minimum treatment and then be discharged.

All employers pay a tax to the government to employ people, and this tax will be abolished. Instead of this tax, all employers will pay for employees and their families, up to a maximum of five per employee, which will be £100 per month. This means that, according to unemployment rates, only 7.4 per cent of people will be without insurance; but those people will be working for the government, so they will be okay as long as they get off their asses and work.

So my county hospital fund will have £5.556 billion; this is £100 per head NI, which, in reality, will be a hell of a lot more than this amount. I will also reduce the tax and VAT on fags to £2 a pack instead of £3.50, and I will put that in the pot as well. So let's say that is another £3.65 billion, worked out on ten million smokers in the UK at ten fags a day; that's £10 million a day.

If we get rid of the NHS, that's £9.206 billion for my funds and already everyone is better off. All we have to do is look at my earlier point that BUPA makes money and many people can pay all their tax and afford private health insurance. I think that in itself proves if the health service was privatised, we would all be happier as a country.

Chapter 13
Different Income Tax Rates

WHY SHOULD THERE BE DIFFERENT tax brackets? My understanding is this: everyone gets a tax-free allowance on wages of say four grand a year. So the first four grand is yours, apart from your NI, of course. Then from £4,000 to £40,000, you pay say 20 per cent plus your NI; then after that, you pay 40 per cent on all additional money earned. Tell me, even if you don't earn enough to pay the 40 per cent, how that is fair. Do you get any more from the country? Do you get any of the advantages that someone on £20,000per year gets? No, so you are in reality being punished for doing well and trying to make a success of your life.

We don't want communism, apparently, so why is the person who tries to do well so badly punished? Simple: because you can do nothing about it! If you earn £20,000per year, you pay 20 per cent of £16,000, but if you earn £100,000, you pay 20 per cent of £36,000, then 40 per cent of £63,000. Let's total that up; your take home out of £20,000 is £16,800 and out of £100,000 is £66,600, so by progressing through life and working your way up through blood sweat and tears, you are losing over 33 per cent of your hard-earned money. That is not taking into account all your other tax; for example, to have a company car, amongst many other things, you get taxed. Surely, if you earn more money, you will already be paying more tax, so why stick more tax on your extra income? Where is the incentive to do well; where is the motivation?

I think this is another tax put in place to support so many things that we don't care about, things that the government feels obliged to support to keep the do-gooders happy. I bet you that, with no knowledge on how to be a cabinet minister (and, by the way, I mean, it's hard to know how you are supposed to be knowledgeable, so you are politically correct instead), I could look at last year's expenditures and make some changes that would benefit us all. After all, this chapter is about why different income tax brackets exist, so I, as a taxpaying citizen, want to find out why. I'm damn sure there is a very good reason behind it. I am not saying that our government is stupid; I'm sure politicians have the same struggles the average businessman has to keep things positive, but they keep forgetting one very huge and important thing: the tax payer. What is it going to take for the government to think about taxpayers? I mean, yes, a total amount of revenue must be accounted for and nothing has drastically changed for so long that the government just robs from Peter to pay Paul. There is no one with anything different to challenge how the budget is spent. All that happens is they give a minor few a matter of pence and then they have to add that on to something else to replace what they are giving away.

Most people reading this chapter think I am for the capitalist, and deep down, you are right. But I, as a person who employs people that I think the world of and have close family that I see struggling every day, care about each and every taxpayer. It's not about the rich getting a break; it's about everyone in our society being treated fairly. I don't believe there are many differences between either party anymore. Gone are the Thatcher years when a very extreme and powerful woman took this country by the balls and made changes that no one had ever dared to make and did things that no one would ever dare to do. I have spoken to many Labour supporters and, although they hated her, every single one of them said this: we had more money in our pockets when she was in power. What a shout! Even though interest rates were at an all-time high, we were still better off than we are today, early 2009. Let's be fair; things look the worst they have ever looked. For someone like me to be writing this book, hoping that it will open the door for us to get a break, says it all.

Going back to my earlier point about last year's expenditure, I want to put it in laymen's terms. Let's say I am Tony Blair; let's forget Gordon Brown, as he took over midterm, an indecency I don't agree with because we didn't vote for him. I think when a prime minister quits, we should have a general election; but forget that for a minute. He was voted in after he publicly went on about the general issues of this country, and we believed, with his skills, he could do something to make the country better. We voted for him, and he became the prime minister. Now he has told all his lies, we have believed his propaganda, he is number one, and we wait with some excitement, as it has been a Tory government for so long. What will this fresh and keen man bring to the table to change this country around radically?

We lived through it, and as I have been saying all along, he brought absolutely nothing new. If I were voted in, knowing nothing of how politics work, which to my mind is the best way because I would have absolutely no bad habits, I would immediately surround myself with all the boffins that can listen to what I say and tell me whether my ideas are viable. However, if they said my plans were not viable, simply because of what they are used to seeing, they had better have a very good reason because I would expect them to start thinking outside the box. I have said all along I am not super intelligent, but I do have great ideas. I would use other very intelligent people to make them happen, as I'm sure the prime minister has the pick of the bunch when it comes to his cabinet and advisors.

So I am voted in, or someone else is voted in with the thoughts of the taxpayer at the forefront of his agenda, what is the first thing to do?

Look at last year's revenue. Say the government had a bank account as we do. On the statement, it says x amount of pounds paid in and x amount of pounds paid out. Judging by the state of the economy, I am assuming that there is a very big overdraft on that account.

So we discover on day one that we are spending more than we are getting in. We have just taken over the country and what a mess we have walked into, although it's not like a real business because we have four years no matter how crappy at running the business we are. If we mess it up, we're not going to lose any personal money, so what the hell. In reality, there are no consequences for our actions. Look at a football manager; if he loses ten weeks in a row, he is fired. That's what I call real life. If that happened in politics, perhaps politicians would try harder.

So if the previous person had been doing his best but spent more than was taken in, what can we do to change things? Well, that is a question. We shouldn't take the job if we don't have some new ideas. Otherwise, and this is reality, nothing will change. It never has, has it?

Once we realise how much we are spending over what we are earning, we then have to look at what the money was spent on. I'm sure we have all been there. So we study the expenditure and instead of charging more tax, we need to cut costs on the things that are a drain on our taxpayers' money. Oh, but everything is worthwhile, you say. No, it's not; when you and I think about our budget, a pound is a pound, so the government needs to stop being so blasé about the coffers. Let's not fly an accused terrorist back to this country from Guantanamo Bay on a private plane at a cost to the taxpayer of £160,000and let the RAF take him back in one of our planes at a cost of fuel and maintenance. How many things like this go on, and who is freely spending this kind of money on a total scumbag that shouldn't even be in our country because his visa has expired? It is sheer incompetence, and it's time it stopped. That is just one example I found in the paper the other day. What a government should do is care about every pound. It should employ people with enough brains to say *no*! If I were to put this to my constituency, what would they say?

To sum up, I will say this. Take me. If I were voted in, I would calculate all the changes I want to make, popular and controversial, into the budget. I would be doing what is right for the taxpayer, for all of us. I would then employ the best money people in the world to make it happen. All you need are *balls*. America has very poor people, and why, you ask? Because these individuals think America owes them a favour, and it doesn't.

I came from nothing, as nearly all of us did. We are all in control of our own destiny. Take the cushion away and make life uncomfortable, and you will soon see people helping themselves. Mark my words.

Chapter 14
Outrageous Taxes

IN THIS BOOK, YOU WILL notice that some chapters are much longer than others are, and some chapters start with relevance to the headline and then digress into great opinions, but opinions that may not have much relevance to the headline. Let me explain. I am not a writer, as I'm sure you have gathered by now. But I have so many things running in my head that I want to get out, that as I think of something, it goes in the laptop. I am sure if I were not so keen to get this book to a publisher so I can see what happens, I could spend months perfecting it. I know my motives for writing it, though, which are honesty and freedom of speech. I may talk bollox, but I wonder how it has taken this long for someone to write the things I am writing, and even more, I wonder what impact, if any, this book will produce. I will be so honest with you that I will tell you this. I took this book, at about 10,000 words, to my dad. My father is the best critic I could chance it with because I knew he would tell me like it is.

His very words to me, bearing in mind I am his only son and he has always pushed me very hard and done me no favours, even though he is extremely wealthy, were, 'Son, you are a genius. I could not have written this, and I am very proud of you, although I think when you release it, MI5 will probably kill you.'

What an amazing thing he said. I thought the book was good, and I was writing it from my heart, but his opinion was the biggest booster I could have ever asked for. Thanks Dad, and by the way, this book shows you that I listened when I was growing up. A lot of my opinions are the ones I heard from you, I bet most of them over a beer in the pub.

Anyway, diverted from the headline again, I am going to pick two outrageous taxes. These taxes, I think, annoy most people in our country; at least, that's what I've surmised from my conversations with the people I know.

The first must be the inheritance tax. I can't remember what the threshold is to avoid paying it; all I know is I had to take out another life policy to cover my loved ones' inheritance tax. What right does the government have to take money from a dead person's estate when he had been robbed of his money in tax all his life? The money I leave, whether life insurance or money that has already been taxed to the hilt, should be paid in its entirety to my beneficiaries. How dare you take money from my grieving loved ones just because it's over a certain amount? How dare you make it 40 per cent? That is nearly half of what I have grafted for all my life to give my children a good head start in life. I know, and everyone else knows, that this is a step too far. I'll tell you this. If I knew 40 per cent would be taken, I would give it to my favourite charity. I wouldn't give it to the government, who will waste it. As I have said throughout this book, politicians don't have a clue what they're doing anyway.

I think the fact that I have pointed this out is so powerful that little more needs to be said, apart from one thing. Suppose I left my children my home that was worth £700,000. I bought the house for £400,000and have a mortgage of £300,000when I die, let's say ten years after I bought it. I am a normal person, so only can only afford life insurance to cover my mortgage on a decreasing basis. I've just died, and after all my debts are cleared and my funeral has been paid (which is £25,000), there is £275,000 to put towards my mortgage of £300,000, leaving a balance of £25,000 to my estate. That isn't expensive for a £700,000 property, but here is the thing. Let's say the nil threshold for inheritance tax is about £300,000, so my estate has to pay £145,000 in tax. Suppose all my family earn the average wage of £25,000 per year; that means they will have to sell that family home I looked after for my kids and grand kids just to pay the government the money it has no right to demand. I bet as well that they will have a time limit to pay it, so they will have to sell my house cheap, let's say for £600,000, to get a quick sale. They pay the mortgage, £25,000 from the sale proceeds, and the estate agent, 2 per cent or £12,000, and then those thieving gits take £145,000. That leaves my family a grand total of £443,000 out of what should have been £650,000! What a joke! How the hell have we been letting this happen since before I was born? I will stop now, because I get myself mad and I bet you guys get mad, too.

The second has to be stamp duty. This just amazes me. Every time you buy a house to better yourself, you have to pay a percentage to the government. You are not claiming benefits, you no longer wish to rent because it's dead money, and so you must make sure you budget a very big amount in tax just for having the ambition to better yourself. In fairness, because houses have gone so sky high recently, the government abolished stamp duty on all properties below £199,000. Well, thanks, oh wise ones; that probably helps all of 5 per cent of the population. In fairness, what first-time buyers do you know that can afford even £100,000 for a house which, where I live, doesn't even exist, or at least very few even on the council estates.

Last time I moved, I sold my house for £200,000 then moved to Bulgaria to do some property development for a couple of years. I had already paid, when I bought that house I sold, £2,625 in stamp duty. Then, when I came back, I rented for a couple of months till I found the house I wanted. I decided I would buy a very expensive project to take a challenge and make a few quid, so I paid £500,000 for the house I have now. That cost me £15,000 in stamp duty, which I will tell you, I didn't have; but you've got to pay it upfront, too. What the hell for? Say now that this house is done up and, even in this climate, is worth £650,000; when I sell it, and of course, I will one day pay another lot of stamp duty on the next property I buy. Surely, I have already paid £15,000 so the next place I buy should be free of stamp duty, or if it's £700,000, I should only pay the stamp duty on the extra £200,000. Oh, no! Let's just take another £21,000. Every time this hardworking taxpaying citizen moves, even if it's his only property and his family home, let's get our greedy, robbing chunk out of the mug every single time. Forget this, guys. Come on. This is madness; this is absolutely crazy.

You must be thinking after every chapter you read, that I am making such amazing sense you need to know more about my plan to change things. Well, don't worry; all in good time, unless of course, you want to flick to the back page and e-mail one of my colleagues your interest. This book is not about pointing out stuff then forgetting what I've said; this is about my passion to change things. I'm at the end of my tether, and I'm expressing myself to my fellow taxpayers in hopes they'll get behind me and help me find the right path to change things for good.

Chapter 15

VAT

VAT IS WORLDWIDE, BUT WHAT a piss take. Along with all the other tax you're paying, everything you buy has 15 per cent put on top and this goes to the government as well. VAT registered companies can claim it back, but what about the end user, <u>you</u>!

You're the one who suffers, but mostly you don't notice because it's hidden in the price of the things you buy. And it's the norm, so why complain.

Let's take a packet of cigarettes, which average £5 to the consumer or end user.

How much of this does the government get in tax and VAT? I estimate about £3.50. Is that fair? <u>No</u>, it's not; they are already getting £3 in tax, but why not steal another 50p in VAT. It takes the piss.

If you are a company that exports to other EU countries, you don't charge VAT on the goods you supply. If you bought £100 of clothes from a wholesaler in the UK, you would pay £115, including VAT. Now, of course, you would want to make money on these clothes, so you put on your profit margin of say 10 per cent. Suppose your customer is based in France. You invoice him £110 zero-rated of VAT; you then claim back the VAT you paid to your supplier from Her Majesties Revenue and Customs so you have in your business account £125, £115 of which you pay your supplier. That means you have turned a gross profit of £10 from this transaction. You pay your overheads, let's say 60 per cent, so your net profit is £4. Then you pay your tax. Let's assume you're a limited company; you are left with £3.20 for yourself, less your income tax on the dividends or wages you draw.

Sounds simple, doesn't it? You are following the rules and paying your dues, so no problem. Think again! There is a little thing in all EU countries called MTIC fraud, or organised trading. This costs the government, on average, three billion in stolen revenue per year. How it works is like this.

The example above, if involved in MTIC fraud, would pay their supplier the VAT. Of course, the value of the transaction would be a lot higher and instead of paying the VAT to the government, the company uses various methods to steal this money and not hand over the VAT.

So the government is stealing from you, and oh no, criminals are stealing from the government. Well, the government can't have that because it is losing £3 billion a year, but let's think about this. How much does the government spend to combat this fraud? I bet it's close to the £3 billion they are losing; so all of a sudden, we are losing £6 billion as a country, and genuine companies are being put out of business every day because HMRC are withholding VAT reclaims in what's called extended verification. This means investigating these matters for years with no time limit at the cost of the taxpayers' money. Let me put this into context: genuine people are losing their livelihood to combat a £3 billion loss to the government.

What about the £60 billion the government spends on paying out benefits?

Surely, it would be far better to pick on a £60 billion loss than a £3 billion one; it's not rocket science. I agree crime is wrong, but that's the world we live in. We must concentrate on the things that can help the people in this country.

Chapter 16
Teenage Pregnancy: Having Children and the CSA

I DON'T KNOW ABOUT PEOPLE reading this book and society in general, but as a taxpayer, I am sick to death of the common attitude of teenage mothers from backgrounds commonly that scrounge from us. They expect the government to fund their intentions to have a baby to get an easy life, in other words, to be supported by us. On the other hand, they expect the government to fund their mistakes, by which I mean they choose to have sex under age, which I have to point out is illegal, with no means to support themselves.

This must stop; the children they bring into this world will be, in most cases, brought up on benefits with no motivation for success. In other words, these children become the next generation of benefit claimers.

What has happened to this country? I agree in times gone by that things may have been harsh for these women, but by all accounts, the government did not encourage this behaviour, which was surely a positive thing as it was much more rare than it is today. This is the problem put very briefly as, believe it or not, we pay for special schools to make sure these girls get an education. What will that achieve? They will find it hard to aspire to anything as they have the responsibility of a baby, which at best is very hard work.

I have three children and two divorces behind me, but I pay for those kids. Why shouldn't I? They are mine and therefore mine to support. My two kids, who don't live with me, I treat like my angels; both girls, they are very clever, not because they have a unique talent, but because their mothers and I are prepared to invest the adequate time in them to give them a chance of a bright future. I wanted them for the right reasons, and that is what makes the difference. Why do people have children? People have children for many reasons, and here goes.

Most people are born with the instinct to procreate, but here is the thing. Sex is what everyone wants initially because that's what our hormones dictate. So at a young age, you are irresponsible; you forget your contraception or something goes wrong and, lo and behold, there is another drain on our tax money. When you reach a certain age and you realise how hard life is, you may make an informed decision that you want to take your relationship further and have a child with the person you love. That will be a decision that you have reached after weighing all the pros and cons of what a baby brings and intending to be with your chosen partner forever.

After my unlucky relationships, I did decide to have another baby and I could afford to make that choice. It was not a luxury; I was in a position, through hard work and determination, to make that choice. My new partner and I have our ups and downs as everyone else does, but all in all, we love each other, think we are forever, and hope to be the best parents we can be for our child. There are many people like me, and good luck to them, because I rightly know what is at stake when you take on such a commitment.

But what about the other side? What about the people who are just careless or the people deliberately don't take that pill or put on that condom? What responsibility do they fear? None, because the hardest thing in life is fighting to do the best for your family, working hard, and giving them the things they deserve. But there is this mentality out there, bizarre as it seems: what can I get if I have a baby, and if I'm twelve, what can my loser family get off the back of me being pregnant? It's a vicious circle we need to break. But how, you ask, how do we break it without going to the lengths of the old days when society looked down at girls who were pregnant with no father to show and no prospects to support this innocent life they were choosing to bring into this world? Here's how! We discourage the whole concept by taking a no-tolerance stance. When a girl discovers she is pregnant, at some point, she has to tell her family; in the scrounging world, most of them are supportive and say, 'don't worry, we will be there for you.' And why? Because it's not their money that's gonna pay for it. If we said as a government that if a mother with no means wants a baby, we are not paying, how many of them would not be so blasé? They'd have no perks for getting up the duff, no happy ending, just what faces every hardworking family that exists in this society. They'd have to worry about how to afford their new little bundle of joy and what dreams to have for their future. Here is the funny thing. If you invest in someone, you have a vested interest in how that person turns out. If you scab, you don't really care. They are just the reason you have a roof over your head and free money in your pocket.

Let me touch briefly on the CSA. Here is another one of those sneaky little ideas from the government to combat the very issues I have mentioned above. Here is the problem; those dregs of society that abuse the system and keep having kids just leave a bigger hole for those people who have a child born in love then split up. The problem is this; you work hard, and a percentage of your money is taken from you at source. If you have one child and earn £100,000 a year, you pay £15,000 for your child; now let's assume your sexual partner got pregnant on a one-night stand and decided to keep the baby to get a better life for herself because that is how easy it really is. She names you as the father, so the CSA contacts you. She claims benefits and, all in all, she will get £10,000 per year. You never wanted the kid; it was a drunken one-night stand. But you lose £15,000 and she costs £10,000, but where does the other £5,000 go? Why are you paying more than your child receives? Where is the logic in that? Who thought of that system?

I'll tell you who, the government! The government wants to pay for that loser, so I know, punishes the guy who works hard and pays a load of tax! Well, not any more. The dregs can suffer because we will not pay for them anymore. How about that? Is that fair, you say? What about those poor babies that might starve? They're not our problem. We didn't decide to bring them into this world with no money, so why should we fund them?

Let me ask you this in closing. What about those children in Africa that are starving to death every day. They have no water, no food, and no basic sanitation. What are your thoughts for them? They have no sex education and no contraception, but don't worry about them. We are not forced to pay for them, so why does it matter? Well, it does matter! Get lost, you scrounging sods if you can't fund a kid. Don't bother getting pregnant, because our money is for us, not for you.

Do you think it's changing?

Chapter 17
Divorce and Custody of Children

LET ME TELL YOU THIS; being divorced twice and with three children, all with different mothers, this has to be my expert subject. However, it's not a subject that interests me. I am only writing about it because I feel for people, more often than not men, because their rights are not deemed to be equal, and that's wrong. Let's take divorce or splitting up with your partner. When you start a relationship with someone, you are both very much individual people, so who is to say that when you split up, whether married or not, you have to split everything you have worked for personally with someone else, just because your relationship didn't work out. I think whatever was yours remains yours. You take it when you split up, so if you own a house jointly and have both paid equally throughout your relationship, you get half each; but if one, no matter whether it's the women or the man, has kept the other, why the hell should that one get half?

My dad has paid out over half a million in divorce settlements in his life. I feel very sorry for him, especially because his second wife, who had nothing when they met, had the life of Reilly then she took over £250,000 when they split up. They have no kids together, but she had him over a barrel, so he paid up. That sucks, and it's time we in Britain looked at it.

Let's move on to custody of children. Why is it that society assumes that the children are better off with the mother? Not only that, but if the woman wants to be awkward, a man may even struggle to get access to see his child; hence, the men that dress up in superhero costumes just to be noticed by the government. It's surely a positive thing for children to have their father in their life, and you can bet your bottom dollar that loving fathers like that are paying their dues to the CSA. The government should help them. What is wrong with you! Let's also give the fathers a fair chance at custody; look at both parents and judge them on their merits. Don't scrutinise the dad if you don't hear his side. How do you know that his child won't be better off with him? It's another example of our leaders needing to put things in place to make our society fair for everyone. This chapter has no relevance to our tax money, but I want all of you reading it to understand that I am not only interested in saving you tax, but I'm also interested in changing things that are very real issues in our everyday life.

Chapter 18
Religion and Terrorism: How Much Do These Wars Cost

I HAVE TOUCHED ON A bit of this chapter in my earlier points, but I feel I may need to reiterate them, even though it may be in a slightly different way. This issue is one about which no politician can ever say his true feelings, whatever they may be. I have a strong and meaningful opinion on this subject, and I don't care what anybody thinks. I know I am an 'each to your own' person with no grudge to bear against anybody; however, I know what is right and wrong, and I know there are very evil people in this world that lie to young men and prey on their beliefs to go to a far superior place. If they perform certain acts, and that is the crime, that is where they fall down. They believe in something far greater than anything they will achieve in this hard and cruel world, so they listen and believe that what they do will be rewarded in the next life.

How sad it is that these men that do these terrible things have a loving family somewhere. They are so brainwashed by these evil people that they would take innocent lives and think nothing of it. Never doubt that what they are about to do is cruel and wrong. So what does anyone do?

It doesn't happen just in Britain and America; let's not forget that most of it happens in their own countries. It is very rare that anything drastic ever happens behind our borders, especially after the two major incidents in America then Britain, as let's be fair, we are red alert. So since the Twin Towers tragedy, which being honest is the first time I remember anything of terrorism apart from the war with the Republic of Ireland, again over religion, we in the Western world have this major fear, and quite rightly so, about terror attacks.

What do we then do about it? We all watch films and see in Hollywood that when our national security is threatened, we go to such extreme lengths to protect it. Why wouldn't we? But from who and what? We, as a united force, have no idea who we are fighting and what they want. Al Queda are apparently the threat; they are always on TV saying what they are fighting for. Well, I, as a British citizen, still don't know. Let's ask them what will make them stop. Imagine if we could all reach a peaceful solution and the killing could stop. Let's negotiate; let's hear them. Maybe they have no other way of making the Western world listen. I say this. No matter what we do to stop these people, we can't win against people who are willing to die for what they believe in. You take out one, and two replace him. It's time for a change in strategy.

One more thing to say on actual terrorism, because let's be fair, you and I could go on all day about this subject. It's time to listen. There are always problems in life; but where there is a problem, there is always a solution.

There has to be very mixed opinions of the cost of these wars and the cost to the taxpayer. All I want to say is this. There is a definite need in today's world to have armed forces, as they have theirs so you have yours. However, aside from the sheer colossal cost of going to war, I really think we should consider, not the money, but the cost of human life. That, for me, is the real cost and I'm damn sure we all agree.

Chapter 19
Council Tax

THE COUNCIL TAX IS THE only bill that, if you don't pay it, you are going to jail. Amazing that this all started as POLL Tax, introduced to my knowledge by Maggie. In my opinion, it's a very good idea. Everyone in our society should pay an equal amount to benefit from the services we all receive, such as the police, the roads and public amenities, fire protection, Coast Guard, and things like having your rubbish taken. Well, shit! Since a little thing like council tax got introduced, how bad has it become. The higher your band is for your property, the more you pay, even though you get nothing more in return for your extra cash. I will be careful here not to write about too much, because most of the things we are supposedly paying for I have discussed in chapters all their own.

But let's take our community and the things we see happening every day and the improvements we see happening. We see changes mostly on the highway, and of course, we will all notice because we spend most of lives in traffic jams because of them. I reckon each and every council gets none of our council tax. I reckon it all goes to the government, who decides, no matter how much is collected from each county, what is given to each council. Then if this council does not spend it, it gets less the following year. This is why I quite often wonder why certain things are being done that in reality have no need to be done, but those efforts get funding. If our council doesn't spend its budget, it will lose money the following year. This system means they must spend, spend, spend. This means that if every council does the same, I mean waste money unnecessarily, our council tax will never go down, and it will only go up. What a joke!

When I said earlier, all we see are the highways getting fixed. Surely, that is funded by car tax, another absolute rip unless we do pay that to keep up the highways and it gets discounted from our council tax. So I am saying that I personally only get the police, fire, Coast Guard, and dustman from my council tax, same as the rest of you. All those things I mentioned above, apart from the dustman, I have never used. Even the bin men are fussy about what they take, so I have to dispose of my own rubbish from time to time. Where does this money really go? I can't do all the work. I will let you consider a very prominent part of your budget, and Christ, it's a lot every month. You decide in your own mind. If you don't get anything back, apart from jail or bailiffs, if you can't afford to pay, where does our council tax go?

Chapter 20
The TV License

THIS IS SO NORMAL THAT I bet no one even really thinks about it. Well, I do. Although it may only be just over one hundred quid a year, this really annoys me. I'm going to tell you why.

Every household pays this license for the BBC, and this includes the radio. This is the law, and you can be fined up to five grand if you are caught without one. You have no choice to opt out, so therefore, you are forced to purchase BBC's programmes, whether TV or radio, and the whole reason and benefit behind this is so there are no adverts on any of their broadcasts. Or are there?

Of course, there are adverts. They advertise their own stuff constantly on the TV. Is that an advert? Yes, it is. I personally only purposely watch *Eastenders* and *Top Gear* on the BBC. As for the radio, what rubbish that is. After listening to those presenters on *Radio 1*, I wish there were adverts to cut the crap they talk (apart from Chris Moyles, who is funny). I must be honest; I don't even have Radio One on my memory stations, as I hate it so much.

So tell me this. We can choose who provides us with TV, such as Sky, Virgin Media, or BT vision, so why must we pay more money for the BBC? Let's be honest. If they disappeared tomorrow, would we miss them? Of course not!

So when we get a decent government, I say we have the choice. If we want the TV bit, we subscribe, and if we don't, we don't subscribe. As for the radio, sell it off to a good radio station. We will have a few adverts, but I would rather not pay one hundred odd pounds per year because that is the government dictating to me what I have to buy. Has anyone forgotten that if you're blind and can't even see the TV, you only get a small discount? What is that about? Eh, sorry, I forgot; you can listen to BBC Radio when you drive to work, so we won't offer you a bigger discount. Not the BBC. They won't listen to it in the car because they can't drive. How the hell is this allowed? Yet another rip off!

Chapter 21
The Brilliant Smoking Ban

THIS WILL BE A VERY split chapter, in the opinions of people reading it, I mean. There are about ten million smokers in the UK, so not even 10 per cent, but Of course , some of the UK population is under sixteen.

I really wonder what the idea behind the smoking ban is, as to my mind, the only thing it has done is destroy the pub industry. As a smoker, I remember when the ban came in. I was away on my cousin's stag weekend at Butlins in Minehead, and the ban came into effect midnight on the Saturday night/Sunday morning. They had to let people smoke into the early hours until the pubs closed, as it would have been a bit silly to announce that everyone had to stop at dead on midnight. So this was new territory, an age-old habit to break. Who could have known that smoking was such an important part of our social rights as human beings and that overnight this ridiculous decision would ruin the lives of so many landlords? The change destroyed their customer base. I myself now very rarely socialise in a pub or club because

I can't relax, as I enjoy a cigarette with a beer, whilst watching the football with my mates.

I agree that it is not fair for a nonsmoker to suffer passive smoking in a public place. If we think back to before the smoking ban, these people had a choice not to go to the pubs or clubs if it was such a major issue for them. Equally so, why should they suffer if it did bother them?

I'll tell you why. If the nonsmokers are such a support to the pub trade, then why are so many pubs going bust through lack of custom? Like it or not, it must be the case that the majority of people who frequent pubs must smoke, otherwise these places would still be thriving.

Why do we have to go to such extreme lengths? I can come up with lots of solutions to keep everybody happy, but I am only going to suggest three. To my mind, it really says something when little old me has to think for our almighty government. I am in this chapter only referring to places where you can buy food and drink, as I am inclined to agree that smoking in public places is not necessary apart from the above-mentioned places. In those places, I feel is imperative that we have the choice.

1. The owner of the premises has to right to choose. This means that he openly displays whether his premises is smoking or nonsmoking. That way, the general public has the choice whether or not to frequent that establishment.

2. If you sell food or allow children into your premises, you cannot allow smoking. This then means the old pubs that have had a loyal cliental for years, people who only go to the pub to see their pals, have a beer,

and a fag with their pint, don't get punished. I'll tell you this. It's the old boys I feel sorry for, when they have had their only vice taken away from them their one enjoyment. A pint and a fag with their mates that they have had all their lives. Who the hell are we to take that away from them?

3. We allow smoking in all pubs and clubs, with a big but. A minimum requirement is put in place for a state-of-the-art air circulation system. I deal in business with many air conditioning companies, and you would be amazed at the efficiency of these systems you can buy these days. These systems can change the entire air in seconds, so in reality, if you only had smoking in one area but the system in the whole place, you would never even smell smoke.

Oh God! I have taken the time to think about an issue from both sides and come up with three solutions that keeps all sides happy. What a proper little diplomat I have become. Once again, all problems have a solution. Let's take time to consider the impact these decisions have on society as a whole.

I must bring up one more thing, I think, in this chapter, and you greens will love this. All the hype over environmental issues and energy efficiency we see every day in the media makes a total mockery of this policy. The government bans smoking in public places, so therefore, forces people to smoke outside. This ban now has created the need for pubs, etc., to implement outside smoking areas. So what you say?

Here in Britain, most of the time, this country is cold. So what do people need while they are having their fag outside? Heat. That's right, electric and gas heaters are going straight outside, using up vital fossil fuels, and polluting the atmosphere. So ask yourself this question. Is the smoking ban better than my three ideas I think not. I'll leave you all to draw your own conclusions. As I said, this is one of those issues that will always be split very evenly. In closing, I will say this: if the government really is anti-smoking and we as a society agree, then make smoking illegal. Marijuana is illegal, and to my mind, smoking fags is far worse. I know the health issues, as we all do, and there is no getting away from the fact that it is bad for you. But people still do it, and that's their choice.

It's human nature to learn from your mistakes. Stop taking away our freedom of choice! It's wrong!

Chapter 22

World Poverty and Corruption

THIS ISSUE IS VERY CLOSE to my heart. Although I have a few quid, I am not rich. I donate a lot to charity and, with Comic Relief coming up, it reminds us all just how bad thing really are in 2009 for so many countries in the world.

Everyone has a charity that they favour, and mine is the plight of the people in Africa. Believe me, all the circulars that come through the door in regard to anything over there I will help, even if I can give only 15 quid. I'll tell you why. The other day, one of these circulars came through the letterbox. It described how a child was carried by his grandma to a hospital ten miles away. As it turns out, he was dehydrated because of the poor quality of the water, so he had the shits. Believe it or not, I am so bad at spelling I couldn't even get near enough to the word we all know, so the spell check couldn't pick it up. Sorry about that.

Anyway, this organisation, the name of which I don't know as it's not a regular of mine, was working to provide this powder that is mixed with water. It rehydrates people, so they don't die. Well, when I read the details, I realised that by making this donation, I would save... wait for it... 187 lives. It gives you a feel-good factor knowing how much a small donation can help. I know that, apart from a few coppers in the charity bottle out of your change, most people don't do much. I'm not knocking you, as I know that in reality, you can't afford it. As I have said before, charity starts at home; furthermore, it is not your fault others are in this situation.

I also want to confess that I give as much as I can afford. Of course, I do so after I have done all the things I want to do, so I am no martyr because of gift aid. This means that for every pound I donate to charity, assuming I pay more in tax than I am donating (and, in fairness, if I didn't, I would be living in a cardboard box and giving half my wages to the government and the other half to charity, as that's how much tax I pay), the government must donate 28p, and that makes me really happy. Anything I can get from the government for something I care about is worthwhile. That is how bitter I have become about politics.

So how the hell are millions of people in the world, in these poor countries, dying every day? *Corruption,* that's how! These people who run these countries are getting away with stealing basic human rights from their people. It's no wonder there is so much civil war going on. But this is a danger, because human greed is devastating and affects all parties involved. What the guerillas started fighting for is forgotten and quickly becomes an even further drain on their countries' resources, because the dictator cannot condone anybody standing up to him. They spend vital funds that need to be spent on people dying on an unnecessary war that would not exist if they had looked after their people in the first place.

I think it will be a very hard prospect to change this scenario, however, until these dictators start to listen. We must take strong action to stop them and cut off their supply of money, unless we see proof that they are using it in the correct way.

Chapter 23
Pedophiles and the Sex Offenders Register

HATE IS A VERY STRONG word, but damn straight, I hate these sick fucks. I bet that the whole of society, apart from pedophiles themselves, hate what pedophiles are and what they are capable of doing. How, I ask you, once they are caught, are they allowed back into society in any capacity? They should be killed. Yes, *killed*, put out of their misery. Let me tell you this. If anybody ever touched my kids, I *would* kill that person. I don't think a jury in the land would convict me. Yes, I would be guilty of murder, but as far as I am concerned, I would have done society a favour. No matter who you are and what job you do, even if you're a copper, you would feel the same.

Children are innocents, and how dare some filthy, sick bastard think they can steal a child's life by doing disgusting things to him. Suppose one of these animals commits a crime. Let's be fair. It's very hard to convict someone of a crime these days, but it is hardly ever wrong when pedophiles are convicted. When a scumbag has done the unthinkable, how dare the very people we trust to police the streets try to rehabilitate these people back into society. If someone has these sick thoughts and desires, that sickness will never leave him no matter what he does. No matter what we do these people, they will exist among us, and we will never know who they are until they are caught.

I have had to have a conversation with all my girls and warn them that if anyone, no matter who they are, ever says to them, 'This is our secret, and if you tell, I will hurt you or your mum and dad,' they must tell me straightaway. I have said to them not to be scared, because I will always be there for them. I have told them that no one will ever hurt you, your mum, or me as long as I draw breath. Never be scared, and tell me everything. The need to do that, in itself, is sick. What has society become that I should have to have this conversation with my precious children just to keep them safe and happy? I'm so scared that something might happen to them, and so protective and cautious, that they need to be told this kind of stuff. I'm not a psychiatrist, but I know that these abusers were more than likely abused themselves, so have had an awful life and pick on children because they cannot relate to adults or sustain an adult relationship. I don't feel sorry for them still, because it's up to them to realise the cruelty they suffered and change it, not ruin more innocent lives.

So what can we do about it? Well, there is a thing called the sex offenders register, and by the way, none of the public have access to this register! The reason for this is simple. If you knew there was a convicted pedophile living near you, what would you do? Only you can imagine. Why does the government not rehabilitate this scum living in our neighbourhoods? Why do you and I have to live near them in our road and without even knowing what they are capable of doing? I take this very personally, and I know you do, too, so this must change. How many times must one of these scumbags re-offend once let out before we tattoo them on the forehead with the word, pedophile?

I say to all the do-gooders that are reading this and even daring to find an ounce of sympathy for these animals, *piss off*. These sick animals are not even human and not worth any shred of compassion. It stops here. I have said what every parent in this world thinks, and I am not afraid to put these offenders in the electric chair. Can you honestly say you are? Remember, it will never happen to you, but say it does. Think about that. Don't wait till it does happen; put a stop to it now. Our children deserve not to worry about these predators, don't you think?

Chapter 24

Police and Their Priorities

THE POLICE, WHAT A JOKE! I have lost all faith in the police, and who could blame me. They have become a load of pompous jobsworths, rude, abrupt, and in the main, very irritating. Their job is to keep society safe, and they spend most of their time picking on the motorist. Well, that is a worthwhile pursuit if ever I saw one. Per square mile, our tiny country has more crime than America. What are we going to do about it? Stop quoting facts and figures because crime has never been so rife. Yet police drive round in their £50,000 BMW X5's pulling people over for being on mobile phones. Our tax money is paying for police vehicles and wages; what is wrong with driving a Kia? Why do the police need a BMW? Police radios help to catch fast cars, so to my mind, it's a waste of taxpayers' money.

Police priorities need to be changed. It's not about figures and targets; it's about keeping the streets safe. So do it! I will drastically cut down the traffic police, who are only pissing off your taxpaying citizens. The rude and abrupt manner of the police annoys me. These silly little Pratts that I am paying tax to employ need to start speaking to the public with respect.

A person is nothing special just by wearing a uniform. Police work for us, and don't forget it. When things in this country change, traffic police will quit because they will have to do the job of a real policeman and fight crime. They might have to chase after a criminal or do something a bit dangerous to get some scum off the street. That's what the public really wants the police for, so they feel safe. There will be no excuse why if some poor person gets burgled, they wait an hour for a policeman to turn up. No more will police be cruising around looking for a broken tail light so they can stick the driver with a fine. Police will be ready to respond to a real crime and support that member of the public that pays for them and needs them.

I have been a victim of crime a couple of times. If I never move from this spot, nothing has ever been done. How many of you could say the same. Some of our police do what I expect as a taxpaying citizen, but not many. I think it's time we had a good look at our protectors' priorities. When will the government understand that we, the taxpayers, live in these towns and cities and see what goes on. It's not about figures, and police are not beating crime. Things are worse now than they have ever been. We are not buying propaganda anymore; do something. I am throwing you the gauntlet.

Chapter 25
Prison Sentences, Justice, and Capital Punishment

I HAVE JUST BEEN TALKING about the police, so let's assume that things change, more criminals start getting arrested, and this country starts moving in the right direction. What then? The justice system is a joke! Where is the deterrent if you get arrested? You know you will more than likely get away with it, and if you don't, the punishment isn't worth worrying about. Even if you murder someone, a life sentence is only fourteen years, and then you get out in seven for good behaviour. Where did fourteen years for a life sentence come from? Who the hell, apart from a small dog, has fourteen years to live? What genius thought of that one?

Your actions, therefore, have no consequence, so why care about breaking the law? Let's be fair. Half the people that break the law would be better off in jail as all the jails we operate are like country clubs. Prisoners have all the mod cons, even TV. How is that punishment? Most people that are in jail will re-offend, as that is all they know. I said before that we need to drastically cut the cost of our prisons. That means we take away all luxury, absolutely everything! If you go to prison, you will not have a two-man cell. You will be in with one hundred people, and you will sleep on the floor with a stinking toilet in the corner. There will be no TV and no gym. Don't let these dangerous people get stronger and bigger; instead, turn them into dithering wrecks, skinny and malnourished. Do you really think they would break the law again? What about human rights, you say? What right do we have to cage someone up like an animal? If society believes that we have the right to do that, then don't make it easy; make it horrible. That's what I call a deterrent. And make the sentence for crime worth thinking about. If you maim someone in a fight because you were drunk, make the sentence twenty-five years. I bet fighting and bad drunken behavior would fall by 99 per cent because there would be consequences. It all sounds so easy when I say it, but have you got the balls to put these things in place? If you had the authority, I don't know if you would. If you could make something happen if you wanted to, if you had the power, how would you feel then? I know my answer, but what about everyone else out there? Unless we are directly affected by misery, we do and say nothing; we act like little sheep in a field. Change it. That's what this country needs.

In closing this chapter, I will touch on capital punishment. This age-old punishment has been outlawed in Britain for quite some time. It was damn right to outlaw it, as back then, we didn't have the technology or capability to determine, outside opinion and circumstantial evidence to prove without a doubt, someone's guilt. However, circumstances are different today. I say it is so difficult to get a case to trial, as you really do need concrete evidence, that if a person is found guilty by a jury of his peers, there should be the option to sentence that person to death. Quite often, this will be the best all-around solution for this dangerous individual.

I happen to believe that the court that convicts that person should not have the power to make this happen. After all, we are talking about someone's life. However, I say once the death penalty has been recommended, the case should be passed to a European court for the final decision. As that court is impartial, it can then review the procedure and decide if this guilty criminal deserves to breathe the same air as we law-abiding citizens or whether he should be destroyed as he is more than likely going to become an expensive pest to society. I refer to America again, where a couple of states have the death penalty. However, they have something called 'death row.' I fail to understand the point of that, as if you are given the death penalty, there is more than likely overwhelming evidence to convict you. Let's not forget, there is no smoke without fire. Why delay? Just get rid of the scum the next day! Why spend unnecessary money keeping convicted criminals alive when they have been handed their punishment? Get on with it.

Again, these comments will leave all readers very split as it is our nature to care about our neighbours. Otherwise, as soon as someone pissed us off, we would be like an animal and just fight till the death with them. On the other hand, I defy anyone reading this to not want to put to death someone who directly harmed either his family or a close friend. Deny this action, and I call you a liar. Don't wait for something to touch your life. Try and feel for your fellow human family and feel their pain. Then reread what I am saying in this chapter and tell me you feel sorry for that criminal who has been convicted, in other words, *proved* guilty, and I guarantee there was forensic evidence. We all watch CSI, so we know the forensics don't lie. If you can't explain what your DNA was doing there, you must be guilty!

Chapter 26
DNA and ID Cards

THIS IS CLEARLY A FOLLOW on chapter from the previous one and has no need to be particularly long. Let's have a debate on whether it should be law to register everyone's DNA. I got arrested once for something I was accused of, a minor argument with an ex. But once I was released, I had to provide my fingerprints and a DNA swab. Obviously, I had no idea if compliance was mandatory as I had done nothing wrong, but why would I not co-operate, as I have not now or never will I in the future have anything to hide. So I, as a decent person in society, had my DNA and fingerprints registered on the national police database. If my DNA, etc., is ever found at a crime scene, authorities will be able to say for sure I was there. That could be blood, skin, hair saliva, semen, or a multitude of things. I'm not bothered, and I feel better for it because as a law-abiding citizen, I will just be eliminated as a suspect quicker. As I said earlier, if someone touched my family, I would kill them. That means I would not try to hide the fact that I was there. I would feel justified in my actions, so therefore, would tell the authorities what happened, and then ask them what they would do.

I have my DNA and fingerprints registered, and I am no threat to society. I say we make it *law*. The only people who won't want this law to happen are people who have something to hide. It's a *fact!* If a murder, rape, or any crime were committed, we would immediately have a suspect because DNA swabbing would be law and the database would point to the suspect. If the suspect were innocent, he would have an alibi. If you are innocent, you have nothing to worry about.

Now I move on to ID cards. I want to tell you about when I moved permanently to Bulgaria. It's an indecently poor country, but they made it very difficult for me to relocate there. Why? I asked then, and you may ask now. I'll tell you, this country is bigger than the UK, yet it has about 5 per cent of the population we have. This country has never even heard of a pedophile, and if a crime is committed, apart from anything mafia related, the authorities are all over it and it is sorted. The authorities know where everyone is, especially immigrants, and they make it their business to periodically check up on them.

When I moved there, I had a tourist visa, a visa C valid for three months. I was supposed to obtain a visa D, which was a permanent visa. I needed it before my visa C expired, but it can only be obtained outside the country. I went through a certain channel to get this and the visa did not come through in time. Although I was employing local people and adding something to their country, immigration came along and told me I should no longer be in the country and I had a week to get out.

This meant moving my family and me out of the country when all my worldly possessions were there until I could get this visa stamped. So a month later back in England, I got this sorted and moved back. Once there this time, I was able to get my permanent visa. My ID card and everything was okay.

What I am trying to say is this. Whoever you are in Bulgaria, you must have legitimate paperwork, and if you don't, you are thrown out of the country. Everybody who lives there has an ID card that, when scanned, tells the authorities where the person is from and what he is all about. This is a very simple scheme to put in place, and I say it is paramount. All our info is on one document; the information is not stuff that people can copy, as it will be irrelevant, but stuff that is needed to establish if that person is up to no good and also where they are. Gone will be the days of people going on the run, as whatever you buy, you will have to swipe your ID card. Really, you will not be able to survive without it. I can hear a lot of you saying, 'But where is our privacy?' Well, you still have it, because you only have to swipe your card when you buy something. Stop moaning. It's for the greater good. If you are not doing anything you shouldn't be doing, you have nothing to worry about, do you?

Chapter 27

Immigration

HERE IS A FAVORITE ISSUE of most people. As I mentioned in the previous chapter, it is very hard for the Brits to move anywhere in the world. So why, you ask, is it so easy for others to move here? The answer is simple. I don't know! All I can say is that, from my experience, if you have nothing to offer, no country in the world will want you. Why would they? However, if you want to come to England, crack on; we will pay for you. I know, why don't you stick in a benefit claim? We will pay it, too! I'm sure you will agree that we want to be a fair society; however, we need to implement a points scoring system so we can decide who and what type of person we want to move here. If you just intend to come here and claim benefits with your huge family, then think again because we don't want you here. I'm not being mean, but I pay tax and I don't want you to put further stress on our very piss taking economy. If you want to come here and you have a trade that we need because we have a shortage of that skill, then please come. I welcome you with open arms.

But if you are fleeing your country to come and claim an easy life from our sucker country, then don't bother because I am closing our borders. I welcome taxpayers, but there are far too many examples of families that were not even born here living a far better life on benefits than most of our working natives, whatever background they are. By this I mean wherever your ancestors came from, whether you be white, black, or Asian, if you were born here, you have as much right to be here as anyone. This common belief, and God, it is true that we are a soft touch, must stop. Do we have a home secretary that is supposedly responsible for this? *Yes!* So what is he doing? He has one job to do in the grand scheme of things. How hard can it be? Once again, I say the only thing you have to think about with this responsibility is the taxpayer. *Stop* giving away our hard-earned money, willie nillie, and do your job!

We don't need the BNP, but slag them off as you will for their extreme stances. They have had enough, like all of us. What does that say to you that a party forms itself and ensures it gets votes on one issue, which in brief is what I am talking about here? What does it say to you that such a party even has to exist? All I can say is fair play to them, well done for having the guts to voice their opinions. I hope you are reading this, because everything the politicians do is there to be challenged. I hope that when this book comes out, all of the parties that are wasting their time trying to win stop and think! Don't concentrate on one thing, like immigration or the environment. Go the whole hog. I really don't see what is difficult about changing things if you are serious and have a plan. We are all human, every single one of us, and the people who are at the forefront of politics should not scare you. They should be scared of you, because you have passion. I'll tell you this. That is really something that should be feared. Someone with an idea and against all odds will do anything to prove he is right is a very powerful threat. We may not agree with religion and the misery it can cause, but this is an example of people who will not stop to achieve what they believe in. How long ago were the crusades, and God forbid, let's not forget the British Empire. We in this country are not whiter than white, believe me, and I want to test the very passion that this country pretends to stand by. I for one see a total mess that is going to take someone completely impartial to sort out. Once again, I think that all the MPs are too out of touch.

Chapter 28
Are My Points Extreme, and Do MPs Even Care?

To BE QUITE HONEST, I have no idea whether my points are extreme or the MPs care. I have written over 20,000 words about our political system, and all I have done is be completely honest.

It really is insignificant whether I am extreme. These points I have made need to be said. If they were not said, we would have no choice but to mosey on through life just moaning about things that bother us. It is my understanding that all I have said does bother us, otherwise I would not have anything to say to you to make you get behind me and do something about it. I wonder quite often if MPs care. As I have said so much through this book, I really doubt that they do. I feel justified in that comment by the issues I have raised.

I would love a chance at running this country. Although I think it is beyond my capabilities, being honest, I really do believe that if I surrounded myself with the right people, I could do a damn sight better job than anyone else in the House of Commons could. I do not say so for any other reason than this. One day very soon, someone who is an MP must say, 'Right. Enough is enough. I can run this country properly because I care enough. I can achieve it!'

In this country, I could name off the top of my head five absolutely amazing business professionals that would be ideal MPs.

Before I name my top five prime candidates for the PMs job, I would like to say one thing.

The following people I mention I like for different reasons. I bet that they meet such shallow people in their life that they miss what makes them special, although I believe I have a sixth sense that makes me a very good judge of character. I feel that despite their superior achievements and wealth, they deserve to be recognised for something unusual. My opinion will in no way affect them or their success, but this is my book and I want to recognise what they mean to me. I will only mention the most important talent that I see. Let's not forget that I don't even know these people.

Number 1 has to be Simon Cowell. I think his talent is his confidence, his foundation for success. He's so sure of his ability to separate who will make him money from who won't and his ability to be honest, no matter what, and no matter whose dreams he destroys. Well done, Simon. I love watching you in action.

Number 2 is Jeremy Clarkson. His humor is his talent. He has a way of telling things as they are and making you laugh. No matter what that guy has to say, everyone would listen. He is the most outrageous guy I have ever had the pleasure to watch.

Number 3 is Richard Branson. I have spoken about this man in my life a fair bit, and I really think that his talent is being likeable. I defy anyone to dislike him. What a legend he is. He's so successful and lucky, and although he is not bad looking, he is no Brad Pitt. But look at his daughter, who is close to being the most beautiful woman on this planet. You are a dark horse, Richard, but the world is a much better place with you in it. Thanks.

Number 4 is Alex Ferguson. He is the most successful football manager of all time. His talent is his strength. He manages the biggest football club in the world, and the players must have huge talent to stay there. However, he is the reason Man Utd are so successful, and no player will ever be bigger than the club will. Even if the fans thought we needed a certain player, if he stepped out of line, Ferguson comes out the one who is right. I respect that strength. It's a breath of fresh air.

Number 5, last but not least, is Theo Paphitas. Although one of my idols, I am not afraid to say I had to search to find the spelling of his name. Apart from being an immensely clever businessman, his edge, and I call it this rather than a talent because I get from him an amazingly strong love for his children! I can't help but notice that, when negotiating, he quite often says, 'You are asking me to spend my children's inheritance.' What a lovely man he is! I could be wrong, but I rarely am about people. I think that he must be a workaholic, but every minute of every day he thinks first of his family. He has reached the point where he cannot fail, but his motives are the purest you can get. His talent is his heart. All the people on *Dragons Den* are amazing in their own, way but I personally think Theo stands out. One more thing. Notice what he invests in; he is a risk taker, although in his position, it may be educated. He will invest in a lot more than anyone else will. I have to agree with him in as much as he is a very sure what he will spend and has very little scruples when it comes to something he wants against the other dragons. You are a very nice guy, Theo. Good luck to you and your family.

I would like to say a special hello to one other person on *Dragons Den* and that is Duncan. Another successful guy, and fair play to you. Well done! I have an insurance broker, and I phoned the person who deals with your insurance for Bannatyne's Health Clubs. I have a scheme with a top insurer for health clubs and, mentioning no names, the person who deals with this was not even interested in what I had to say. As someone who loves to make money, what I have said must piss you off, because I'm not short of a few quid, but will always listen to what someone has to say if it will save me a few quid or make me money. I personally phoned your clubs, and I can save you a minimum of 30 per cent. Next time I phone, because you are in my prospect list, please tell your person to listen. Sales calls are annoying, but sometimes they are important.

So let's get back to this chapter. Am I saying that the above people I mentioned could do a better job? Of course I am, although they do not have time to run this country. This means that the best qualified people apparently have no time, so we settle for Gordon Brown.

Well no! I will make the time, Gordon, so maybe for once, you will have some stiff competition, old boy. I am serious about my beliefs, and I feel I am closer to what matters than you will ever be. Maybe you should have replied to my letter instead of thinking you were to above me. I say you have messed up because you don't care, and I reckon I have exposed you. If I market this book properly, you will have to read it. When you get to this page, believe me, your days are numbered. I believe you will realise that fact. I don't think your kind have ever been challenged like this before. I look forward to seeing you on some programme defending yourself against what I have said, because no matter how much you dismiss it, I will be in your face every single day. I know that the people of this country will be behind me.

Say no more apart from the fact I was going to be an anonymous author, but that would make me as bad as you are. I want to stand up for what I believe in, because that is what this country is all about. So I will go on this morning with you sitting opposite me. I will argue with you because you think you are of superior intelligence to me. You are probably right, but when you try to make me look stupid with your superior vocabulary, I will ask you every time to explain everything I don't understand. I know your game, and you cannot win. I care! None of you greedy, selfish pigs do care, and I will prove it before MI5 say any different. That is the only way you can stop the people of this country. We are taking it back.

Conclusion

BEFORE I WRITE MY CONCLUSION, I wish to print the last letter I wrote to the prime minister. In it, I expressly asked for a reply with his opinions as to my points and got none. His silence made me snap and start to write this book. Now you have read this book, you will notice that, although the points are minimal, they stay true to my beliefs. Obviously, there is more in this book because I decided to put most of the things down that bother me. If only the guy had had the respect for me, a taxpayer, and had taken the time to look at my points and perhaps given me an answer, I wouldn't have had to go to this extreme to try and be heard.

Dear Gordon

I would like to start this letter by saying that I realise that pleasing everybody must be difficult. Please understand that my comments are not directed at you and how you do your job, because in truth, if we were honest, whoever was sitting in your chair would never make the radical changes needed to support the people who grease the wheels so this country can run.

I am very interested in politics, but not for the same reason that MPs are. I will never break into your world because I will never be in a position to be heard. Our country is a democracy, supposedly; but in reality, only because we chose who makes the decisions and then you still have to get everything past all those people in parliament. I always wonder why the Liberal Democrats bother trying to compete with the same policies as the top two, maybe changing a few things here and there, as they will never ever get in. It will always be the Tories or Labour.

Firstly, the main thing you always go on about is the NHS. Why don't you get voted in again by suggesting that we privatise it? I have private health insurance, which I'm sure you do, and, for our family of five, it's about £100 a month. I bet if you took the ridiculous cost out of your budget and made everyone pay for insurance, the average man in the street would be so happy and would have more money in his pocket. Listen when I say this. That's what people want. This is free advice from someone who hears the truth from real working people. Of course, if you suggest this, you will be laughed at. But then, you say it works in the U.S. and look at the working man's standard of living over there compared to ours, look at fuel, look at the standard of their houses…

Before I go on, I am voting Tory and not because I think they are better than you are, but because David makes me laugh. I can almost see him as someone I could have a beer with. He's got balls. But the sad truth is that if he gets in, nothing will change because you guys are too scared of doing something in case it upsets all the leeches of society that live in the north because that is how you get voted in. Let me talk about the £80 billion that unemployment and benefits cost us. I have had enough of paying you over £70,000 in company and personal tax for these losers to get free money.

Here's what you do.

You means test before you have a child. Sounds radical, but for teenage mothers or people with kids, it's too easy to go and have a kid. Too easy when we put them up in their own flat and pay them to sit on their asses all day. Sorry, but it's time to stop.

If someone is unemployed, then instead of sitting on his ass, he works for the local council picking up rubbish, cleaning graphite off walls, or doing anything that needs doing, like community service. If he doesn't do it, he doesn't get benefits. Do you really think someone will work forty hours for 50 quid a week? I bet our unemployment goes down the first week this policy is implemented. I bet teenage pregnancy disappears. If these peoples' parents had to pay instead of me, they would stop their kids getting pregnant in the first place. And, God, if they had to pay for their own abortions, they might make their kids use a condom, because there would no longer be any reward for having a baby.

I don't know whether you agree with anything I've said, but please have the decency to reply. If I'm wrong and these issues don't matter, then I want to hear your opinion. I respect the hard work you have put in to get where you are, but put yourself in my position. Everything I earn I pay you 40 per cent. I have worked hard for what I have. I have been through divorce because of it. If I didn't pay you so much, I would be very well off. I have had enough of being punished because I want to do well. Is it fair? *Really?*

The people I feel sorry for the most are the people with a job. It's so true that this means just over broke. Surely, if you take my comments on board, you can see that it's impossible to live in this country the way things are.

One more thing. Close our borders. I read in the paper the other day that an Afghan family is costing the taxpayers nearly £170,000 per year. That's more than I earn! Let's get real. If you care about your people, you need to forget what you think you have to do to get voted in. You are in a position to make a difference, so do it. Take responsibility for the job you have been given.

I look forward to your response,

Kindest regards,
Scott Mackenzie

P.S. If you ever want to know the real issues, give me a shout. I would be happy to talk to you.

NO REPLY HAS EVER COME. Now coming to the end of this book, I understand why. Writing this and putting my thoughts down on paper, I have learnt a great deal about the very things that bother me. Not because they were not already in my head, but because when you read something over and over and share it with friends and family, you find out that you are not alone. Every single one of us that pays tax in some fashion feels let down by our system.

We are the backbone of this country, each and every working, taxpaying individual. Come on. Let's take our country back and make it good for everyone.

We choose to live in a democracy, so if your neighbor has more money than you do, so what. Maybe he has worked harder than you have or has taken more risks.

The fact is, you and they should stand united and shake the envy, because let me tell you, when they pay their tax, they feel just a sick as you feel. The only winners in this country at the moment are the politicians, the scroungers, and the immoral.

Action Plan

Calling all people who have real ideas for the people of this country!

If you are interested in taking our great country back and you have the means to support the launch of a brand new political party to take on these fools

Join

The Peoples Party

And let's create a new fair future for all the people who built and fought for this country.

It sounds impossible, but I guarantee you that if you give the taxpayer more money in his pocket, he will back us all the way.

Email your interest to:

jointhepeoplesparty@yahoo.co.uk